A Match in Dry Grass

10 Days of Revival in Nairobi

Dalen Garris

Dalen Garris

This is a work of history. Historical individuals and places and events are mentioned.

Copyright © 2021 by Dalen Garris

Cover Design by Renee Garris

Published by Revivalfire Ministries

ISBN 10: 978-1-7377944-2-4

*All rights reserved.
No part of this book may be used or reproduced in any manner whatsoever, without written permission, except in the case of brief quotations embodied in critical articles and reviews, as provided by U.S. Copyright Law.*

For information, address
dale@revivalfire.org

First paperback printing October 2021

Printed in the United States of America

Epilogue

In 2004, the Lord showed me a vision:

I saw myself standing at the edge of a vast field of wheat that reached across Africa from Kenya to Nigeria. The grass was tall, about mid-thigh, and it was dry. So dry that it had turned white and was so brittle that it would crumble in your hand.

I watched myself as I stepped into the field, strike a match, and drop the match into the dry grass. The field of wheat exploded in flames, burning from one end of Africa to the other. As I stood there watching the flames, the Lord spoke to me clearly and directly, "That's my people in Kenya."

God was about to send the fires of His last, great revival across Africa that would burn like a raging fire,

. . . and it was going to start by striking a match in dry grass.

Dalen Garris

Table of Contents

Introduction .... Error! Bookmark not defined.
Saturday, Day 1 4
Sunday, Day 2 8
Monday, Day 3 11
Tuesday, Day 4 16
Wednesday, Day 5 27
Thursday, Day 6 – The Orphanage 38
Friday, Day 7 45
Saturday, Day 8 53
Sunday, Day 9 58
Monday, Day 10 68
Conclusion 70

Stepping into the Field

I'm sitting here in Zurich, Switzerland, on my way to my 3rd journey to Kenya. As usual, there's a great apprehension that has come over me and I am wondering what I am doing. This always happens to me just before I begin a journey – I feel like a fast-flowing river has carried me along and all of a sudden I am waking up to the fact that I have just floated downstream. How did I get here? What am I doing? What is going on? Why am I doing this?

Since these doubts always come after I'm already in motion, it's always too late to do anything about it. Oddly enough, it always seems to be a sign that the journey is of the Lord.

I have no agenda, no set of prepared messages, no organized plan. I'm just going to show up and let the Lord lead the way. The brothers that are there probably have a schedule that is packed out with all the places that

Dalen Garris

I am supposed to go to, and if they don't, I'm just as happy standing on a street corner in downtown Nairobi with a handful of Gospel tracts waiting for the next adventure to open up.

Actually, I'd really like to try something like that one of these days just to see what would happen. I love surprises! I am still nurturing an idea of getting dropped off at a little village in Tanzania to spend a week there– reading Bible with the people, holding prayer meetings, and taking them witnessing in their village – and end the whole week with a big service to bring in souls. Then hitchhike to the next town and do it all over again. After 2 or 3 months in that area, lighting a fire in each village, what a blaze you would have! It would set that whole area on fire, and that fire would most likely spread to the areas around it. What a terrific adventure that would be!

For now, however, this will be a quick 10-day visit in which most of my time will be spent with a very small, brand-new church to help get them up and going. This may be my "test case", so to speak. If the principles of revival work here, they will work anywhere.

And if they will work anywhere, surely it will work in America.

My hope is that an outpouring of the Spirit of God will ignite the Christians in America to rekindle a deep hunger to see the same kind of raw power in a Holy Ghost revival like we have seen not too long ago.

Maybe I'm asking too much, but hey, this is God we're talking about, and the last time I checked, He can do anything.

Once I arrive, dinner is waiting at Mama Puritt's. This is an African custom that is not pressed upon you, but neither is it optional. Everyone gathers around like excited kids ready for an adventure. They are expecting miracles in the next 10 days, but I just want to get some sleep. That's the only miracle I want right now.

Saturday, Day 1

Two things always stand out in Nairobi – color and dirt. There are plenty of both, and somehow the contrast seems to go together well.

These people love color. A snapshot of any crowd will produce a riot of reds, yellows, and greens, set off by bright whites. They are drenched in a symphony of color, rich in sensory tone and visual contrast. It is the visual music of the African soul.

Whatever their personality traits that you may see on the outside, this is something that comes up from deep inside them. It's something that I can sense, but as a white guy that can't dance, I will never be able to fully grasp. The dirt, however, is ubiquitous – from the roads and alleys to the blanket of dust that covers the whole city like a muted haze. The dullness of this reddish-brown dust makes the colors you see in the people all that brighter – almost as if the dust is the canvas that the culture of this bright and colorful people is painted upon. It would take a poet to say it the way it should be told, but hopefully you get the picture.

This dance of contrasts in Africa speaks to something in their soul which not only rises to meet overwhelming challenges in their lives, but to use those challenges to build strength into their spirit. It's hard to explain, but it may be that the enormous challenges they face are their biggest blessing.

The little congregation that I have come to visit here has been facing its own challenges and I have been able to witness one of their first great victories. For months, they have been meeting in someone's home, but that has imposed limitations upon them and they are ready for their own place.

I didn't expect that I would be the catalyst that would precipitate a new church, but they have been waiting for me to arrive before taking the next step. Today's primary goal is to find a place to hold services. They have found a small room to have services in but have been waiting for my approval before renting it. They had already started in the neighborhood passing out Gospel tracts that have given the location and time of tomorrow's service -- and they don't even have the place yet! Talk about faith! Or is it just an African substitute for presumption? Either way, we have to rent a place today or we will be out of luck for services tomorrow.

It struck me later on how easy this has been – we started a church with a vision, a little bit of faith (or presumption, depending upon how you look at it), and a few shillings. And the next day, just like that, we have a church.

Great works of faith, I believe, are accomplished with a determination to succeed and a willingness to take chances, just as much as they are established by faith and belief. You can believe all you want, but at some point, you have to be willing to take a chance, push through to your dream, throw caution to the winds, and just go for it! The worst that can happen is that you will fail, only to get up and try again. I have noticed that when the Lord is in something, it happens cleanly and decisively, and this is one of those times.

So here we are. These people have no money, no equipment, not even any chairs, but they have a church. I believe that God bestows special blessings on a faith that has the courage to believe God and press their vision upon Him like that. It is difficult for those of us who have had everything freely handed to us to fully understand the glory of winning the victory after facing these kinds of challenges. The process forges them into

Christian soldiers with the hardness of iron faith and a determination to do great things for God.

It also makes them capable of believing God for miracles. They expect the supernatural because they have won that birthright through the desperation and the necessity of reaching Heaven for sustenance. They just plain need God more than we do, while we are like the Church of the Laodiceans in our lack of desperation. And that's what makes the difference.

There is one more thing that they have that we don't – their overcoming victories have given them a zeal that builds the fire that is upon the altar of their hearts. Each victory encourages them more, and stokes up the fire's intensity.

We will see how this all plays out in services tomorrow.

Sunday, Day 2

Today is our first day in the new church building. First days always seem like they should be the harbingers of what is to come, so I am a bit anxious to see how the day will turn out with all the obstacles that are facing us.

I have a lot at stake here. Besides the money that has been spent to get here, success or failure will reflect on whether or not I have been led of the Lord in this venture or if I have been just kidding myself. Last night, I was loaded down with fears that this whole trip was a waste of time and money, that nothing would ever come of it, that it was only for the benefit of a very few people, and, because I had touted this as being something important from God, that I was in actuality nothing more than a fraud. Yeah, you-know-who was sitting on my shoulder yakking in my ear. It took a bunch of prayer to shake off the ol' devil and resign myself to the fact that regardless, I am here, and we are going forward no matter what the devil would like to tell me.

I'd like to take the credit for standing up against the devil's accusations, but honestly, the thing that really broke this spell was the idea of my wife rolling her eyes at me if she could have heard all this nonsense.

I thought that we had two services, at 9 am and 1 pm. No, services <u>start</u> at 9 am and <u>continue</u> until 1 pm. This is Africa, not America, and a couple of hours in church are not enough.

We will start with an <u>hour</u> of prayer, followed by a time of praise, and then a message from the Word. Next, we will have members stand up to give testimonies to what the Lord has done for them, followed by some time of worship (distinguished from praise), followed by another message from the Word. Finally, we will close with an altar call and prayer.

Sounds pretty impressive, doesn't it? There are

only 8 people in this church and there is no telling if the tracts we passed out yesterday will reap in any others, so we may have a very slim turnout, but none of that matters to them as long as God is there. This is how great things are started, when the only thing that is big is your faith in God.

Sure enough, the people started coming in until there were about 30 of them. But more than that, the Holy Spirit showed up -- and brother, did He show up in power! For five hours, we were drenched, we were excited, we were shouting and yelling, we were convicted, we were jumping up and down singing at the top of our lungs, and we were in love.

When it was all over, I had that feeling like I had been plugged into an electrical outlet and had been totally drained, used, and satisfied. I needn't have worried that anything about this trip would be inconsequential or vain. We had touched the Throne of God and that is all that matters.

Monday, Day 3

What a day of running this has been! After walking what seemed like miles this morning, I finally made it to the Bible Society of Kenya to pick up the Swahili and Kikuyu Bibles. We had to walk for miles through masses of teeming humanity to get there (which was a whole lot better than attempting to drive there, although not by much).

Driving in downtown Nairobi is like rampaging through a war game of bumper cars with crazed maniacs. The streets are filled with minivans-turned-buses driven with total abandon by young street hustlers fighting for the next fare. There are no rules, and apparently no fear of consequences. If it means driving at top speed down the wrong side of the road right into oncoming traffic or cramming 4 lanes of vehicles into a two-lane street, or jumping the curb and running straight down the sidewalk, then whatever it takes, they will do it. This is offensive driving, not defensive, and if you want to keep from getting smashed up, you have to drive like you mean it!

That's why we were walking instead of driving.

And don't worry about the pedestrians, because they are walking all over the streets like teeming masses of humanity poured over the traffic like syrup on pancakes. When you are in the midst of it, you feel like you're in a fire ant mound that has been stirred up.

It's not just the number of people – "people, people, everywhere" to quote the Ancient Mariner – it's the confusion of swarms of humanity running in every direction. Just like the driving, you have to walk like you are driven with an intense mission, through the crowds, up on the sidewalk, into the street, around the automobiles, back on the sidewalk, back on the street, around this group and through the middle of the next… It is not for the fainthearted.

Once armed with our Bibles, however, we were

off to our first service. This is a lunchtime service, and I've been asked to preach there for the next 3 days. Did you ever hear of a "lunchtime" service? (Invite your neighbors over for lunch – I love it!) They are not uncommon here in Kenya, and that should give you an idea of how hungry these people are for God—services in the middle of the day with loudspeakers broadcasting the service out into the surrounding streets. Try that in the States and see how far you get!

The place is packed, and I'm asked to give a short 15-minute message as an introduction for the next few days. This bishop is interested in building up to a crescendo in the next few days, even to introducing me to the newspapers, the mayor, and some sort of government agencies. He's talking so fast with that Kenyan accent that I have no idea where he's going with this idea, but I warn him that I may not be the little darling that he thinks I am. I have this uncomfortable habit of challenging the ecclesiastical "powers-that-be"

and have made a strong stand against the corruption that is rife in the leadership of the Kenyan church.

He pauses. Then he gets up and excuses himself. Oops. I think I might have hit a nerve, and the deal is probably off. Oh well, perhaps that is just as well. I'm not much for that kind of publicity and attention anyway.

But no, that's not the case at all. In fact, this bishop is extremely aware of the corruption in the Kenyan ecclesiastical circles (after all, he's right in the middle of it), and he is thrilled to hear someone make the stand I have made. He wants to promote this to the hilt and attack this problem head on. I'm not sure what he is planning, but I will just have to leave that in his hands. I've got 10 days here and very little free time to add anything new to the schedule.

As soon as the service is over, we are off to the first of several open-air services. Have you ever been in one of these? Very simply, you plug in some speakers and a keyboard and start singing. In no time at all, you have a crowd dancing in the streets. Give a message, call them to the altar for Salvation, and close with prayer for individual needs. This is as simple a formula as you can come up with – if they won't come to church, then take church to them.

Street preaching, as we call it back home, is not that effective or popular in America, but it works great here. The songs turn this whole area into a block party with dancing in the streets, kids running around wild, and people all over, hanging out over their banisters and sidewalks to listen and have fun. Hey, whatever works!

We prayed through several people, including a whole pack of kids, handed out Bibles, and invited them back to read Bible with us tomorrow afternoon. I'm told that as the meetings continue on, more and more people respond.

This may turn out to be quite a week if that is so.

Tuesday, Day 4

We have started the day with more witnessing. I purchased a stamp to put the name, location, and phone number for this new church on the back of all the Chick tracts that we are passing out.

The Chick tracts are in Swahili. I don't know what they say, but I know how people can't help reading these little comic books. Sure enough, as we walk through the neighborhood, everybody wants one. Kenyan people are very social people, and in no time at all, these tracts will be passed around the whole neighborhood. This is the best advertising there is.

Kids swarm me wherever I go. Could it be because yesterday I bought a big bag of candy to hand out to them? Maybe, but a lot of it is because I'm the "mzungu" (the white guy). I stand out like a white neon lightbulb, and they all want to touch me, rub the hair on my arms, and yell and holler at me.

"How are yooo? How are yooo?", they keep yelling at me in their lilting British-African accent. I guess that's the first English phrase they learn in school. Kinda like "Comment-allez vous?" which is about all I remember from six years of French.

We are out of tracts quickly, and it is time to run off to the "lunch service" in Nairobi. All sorts of people show up here to get a little bit more of God during their lunch hour. Talk about a receptive audience, they are primed and ready for anything and everything they can get from me. Everyone is excited and wants to shake my hands after the service. I don't remember what I said, but I'm not sure it matters. Just the fact that I am here is a thrill for them, so whatever I preach, they will listen to and hold it close to their hearts. You can't want for anything more than that.

After services, it's back to where we will hold another open-air meeting. While they are setting up the equipment, I sit on a stool by the side of the street and start reading Bible with whoever wants to join in. It doesn't take long before we have a sizeable group, all taking turns reading a chapter. I think the thing that really gets me about this is that all I have to do is sit down and open the Bible for them to come. Nobody ever does this for them, especially white evangelists from America, but it's the thing I love the best. To me this is the Christian's idea of a party – get a case of Coke, open your Bibles, and talk about God.

Taking each passage slowly and explaining it in simple terms has the effect of bonding this group closer together. The quiet, shy reticence that is their usual demeanor thaws as we walk through the Scriptures. Soon I am in the midst of a crowd of friends, laughing together as I act out some of the scenes we are reading. This is really a lot of fun.

The amplifiers are set up and interrupt our reading group. An invitation to come to services is broadcast to the whole neighborhood. Sitting right next to the speaker like we are, we got the message loud and clear.

Once the music starts, there is no stopping the celebration. People are clapping and dancing all over the place. These people love music, and the Gospel music draws them in from all over the place. I feel a little bit like we are setting out bait to lure them into our "trap", but they already know the score and they don't care. Open-air preaching is something that happens quite a bit out here.

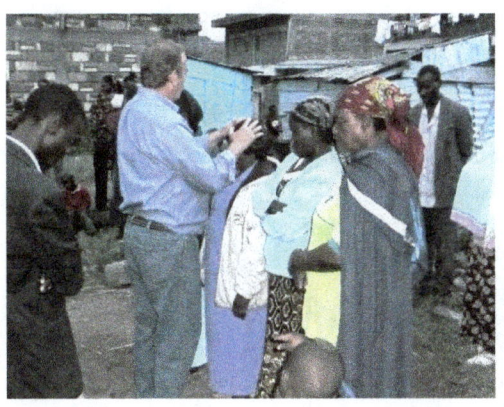

I am results-orientated, and sometimes I feel like I am a little too clinical or mathematical, but I want to see souls get saved, the sick get healed, and the Gospel of Jesus Christ be manifested. I shouldn't have worried about what would happen here because when the Altar Call is given, people start coming ... and keep on coming, even after services are over. This is the proof of one's ministry – winning souls and bearing forth fruit.

People come up to us with all sorts of needs, and we fill every one that we can. We have run out of Bibles to give out, and that is with trying to make sure that they are only given to those who really need them. The

English Bibles go first, then the Swahili and Kikuyu. What a feeling of fulfillment that we get! I know that long after I am gone, those Bibles will be working on these souls with all the power of the Gospel to establish the kingdom of God. I don't know how far they will reach, but I get this feeling that in Heaven I will meet people who were rescued and saved from those Bibles.

Ain't God great?

I am drained, and the picture of my bed back at the hotel is beckoning to me, but it is not to be just yet. We drive to some new area that I've never been to before and I am asked to park.

"What's going on?"

"Services, of course!"

"What services? What happened to the picture of my bed?"

"You have to preach here tonight. The people are waiting for you."

"What people? Why are they waiting for me?"

Surprise, surprise. I am not prepared, have no

message, and I feel like all the messages and Bible have already been poured out of me. But there is nowhere to run, so I have to grin and bear it. My only consolation is that, if I can't deliver a message that is in the Spirit, at least I can run out the back door and nobody will see me again.

Again, I shouldn't have worried. This is not about me. It never was about me, and it is not going to ever be about me. It's about God, and He has an inexhaustible supply of messages in His pocket, and He gives me one of them as I walk in the door.

I am excited as the message pours out of me. Funny, I've never used that expression before, but that's exactly what it is like. You tip the pitcher, and it comes pouring out of you, straight from God, and when the Spirit is flowing, it takes control over the message. I rarely even know what I'm going to say next – I just let it flow.

These people are also excited because they can

feel the power of the Holy Ghost descend in this room. There's something in the air that you can't see but you can feel – almost like invisible electricity. You don't have to be a genius to realize that God is here – right here! -- filling up the entire room.

Then, halfway through the message, I feel the power of God crash down on me with a word from God for this congregation. It is so strong that I physically shuddered right in mid-sentence. They felt it come down too, just as if God had clapped His hands. It is a challenge that is dropped on them straight from the Throne of God, and they sit there, eyes wide and mouths open because they know it!

Wow, what a service! And I thought I had nothing to give them ... well, actually that's true. I didn't. God did. And that made the difference. They will never be the same.

It is late. I'm exhausted but the pastor wants us to come to his house. (Oh please.) He must be pretty excited because he has shaken my hands about five times now. His wife has made dinner, and this is a tradition that you dare not refuse.

So, we squeeze into his tiny apartment. There are hundreds of these housing projects in Nairobi, made of crude block and rough mortar, inside and out. Even the counters and walls are made of coarse concrete. The rooms are so compact that it is difficult to squeeze more than 4 or 5 of us into the living room. It's a good thing we're all friends because we are practically sitting on each other's laps.

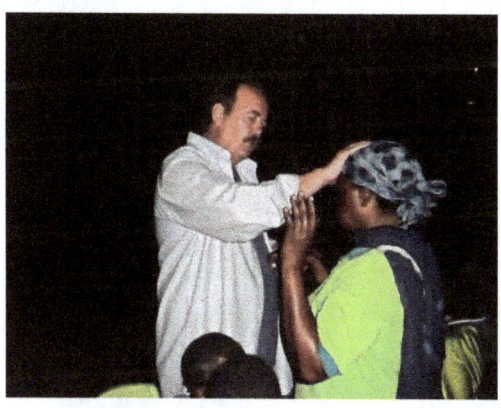

As usual, we share our experiences and what God has shown us for the church. This pastor, like so many others, started with nothing but a dream. Knocking on doors, he gathered a small congregation and built it from there. This is how it is done – a vision and a willingness to work that vision. As we leave, they introduce me to a lady who is sick and is asking for prayer. She has come because she had heard that the prophet from God was here and she expects a miracle.

It's hard to explain exactly how they look at me,

but it is close to celebrity status, and wherever I go they treat me like royalty. A lot of it has to be because I am from America. You have no idea how huge that looms in their eyes: America, The City on the Hill, Land of the Free (and the rich).

But there is also a belief that I have come from God, which is pretty much true. To them that means hope. Hope is in such short supply here that even the faintest glimmer will spark a fire in them to reach for it, and when they see me, they see hope. It's not me, but it is the desperate hope that God has not forgotten them and has taken the time to send someone to them to encourage them in the Faith. It's a sign from God that life may have passed them by, but God has not.

As I stand up and put some oil on my hand to pray over her, I feel like I have just entered into a cloud. Something is about to happen; you can feel it. As I lay hands on her, it is as if someone just threw the switch and the power just turned on. Wow. This quiet lady, who has sat there without saying a word or hardly even lifting her eyes, has just turned into a dynamo. Her hands fly up into the air, she is praying at the top of her lungs, everybody in the room is up on their feet praying and shouting at the top of their lungs, and the power is turned on!

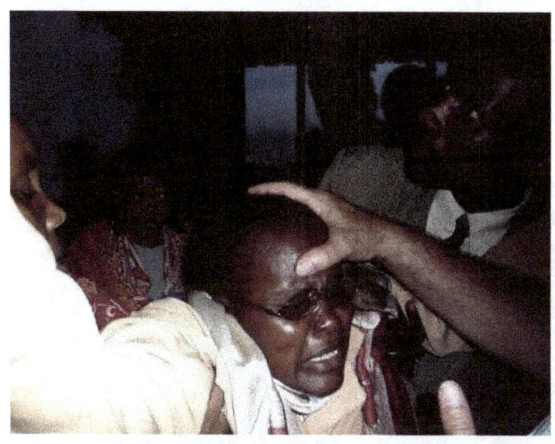

As for me, I'm standing in the middle of all this, and I can feel the power flowing through me into this lady. It is like hanging onto a team of wild horses trying to stay on the saddle. We are all shaking and vibrating, praying like we could wake up the dead, and jumping up and down with excitement. Whew! God has entered the building!

Now, I'm not sure what was wrong with that lady. Their accent is hard for me to understand, so I usually only catch half the words most of the time. They explained it to me, but all I could understand was that she was sick.

Well, she ain't sick no more.

And although I am no longer tired, I do feel

drained. It's as if a torrent has rushed through me all day long, and this last thing was like a dam burst and drained whatever was left. I'm excited, but I am drained.

It is close to midnight when I finally reach the Guest House, and my biggest worry is that I am going to forget some of the things that I want to tell you, but it will all have to wait until tomorrow because I am going to bed.

Wednesday, Day 5

Mornings in Kenya have a fresh tropical smell that is great. Even though Kenya sits right on the equator, it never gets very hot here and it never gets very cold. Texas is actually hotter than Kenya. This is perfect weather, and I am going to soak up as much of it as I can this morning.

I have no meetings until 1 pm, so I am lounging in the lush grounds of the Anglican Church Guest House. I've met some interesting people here that have come from several different parts of the world. Africa, Europe, and Katmandu are just a few samples of the eclectic mix that meets for breakfast. I tell them I'm from Texas, and out here everybody loves Texas, so of course, I play it up for them. "Howdy, howdy", I say to one couple, and a guy at the next table asks me if that is some kind of greeting. Oh boy, this is going to be fun.

Soon enough, however, it is time to charge into

the battle of Nairobi traffic. It has been said that if you can drive in Nairobi, you can drive anywhere. Drive? Is that what you call it? More like a cross between a video war game and a pinball machine. As I enter the melee, it feels like I'm in a shooting gallery and I look like a duck.

There is nothing sacred, fair, or reasonable to the Matatu drivers in their minivans, but they are the backbone of transportation for the public. For a few shillings, you can get to any location throughout Nairobi and its suburbs on these matatus, and get there fast. As crazy as their driving is, their routes are well organized and the system works great.

But they are crazy. They will charge down the wrong side of the road right into oncoming traffic, and somehow never get hit. There is some kind of weird flexibility to the traffic that gives and takes as they jostle through the ever-present traffic jams. A couple of times I have seen a traffic cop get upset at a particularly crazy driver and beat his car with his baton, just like an angry parent with an incorrigible child.

I am praying constantly that my rental car doesn't get smashed up in all this insanity. I'm driving on the wrong side of the road in the middle of a war zone in a car where the controls are backwards. I have learned, however, that the only way to stay alive is to drive as crazy as they do. "Outta the way! Crazy white Mzumgo behind the wheel!" Believe it or not, it works.

Today is the last of my "lunch services". The service goes fine, but there is no supernatural crashing down from the Throne of God. They just sit there on the edge of their chairs soaking up the message. I guess that's what the Lord has for these folks because that's what He has given me. I don't control the message or the results. I'm just the guy who showed up. The rest is up to God.

Today's schedule is pretty much the same as it has been the last three days, so I have to hotfoot it up to Kariobangi Estate for a Bible reading group and another open-air service. Just like before, all I have to do is plop down a stool in the middle of the street, open my Bible, and people come. In no time at all, we have a small crowd taking turns reading. They must have liked the reading group yesterday because they have all returned and have brought friends.

Theirs is a very open community. There's not much for facilities, garbage is piled up everywhere in huge ugly mounds, the streets are rutted dirt roads with huge potholes, and many buildings are only half-finished because the contractor ran out of money. It is a depressing, dirty landscape, but no one seems to notice. Either they just don't care, or they have lived with it so long they can't see it anymore.

But at the same time, there is a feeling that this is a real neighborhood, like something we had back in the '40s. People are hanging out everywhere, some lighting up a BBQ, others sitting in a circle playing dominoes, or just walking home – they are outside interacting with their neighbors, and it feels like a real community.

When it's time to start services, it begins to rain. Pastor Kibedi is proclaiming over the loudspeakers that

God is going to turn away the rain, and he rebukes it in the name of Jesus. I'm a little squeamish about proclaiming stuff like that, but hey, this is Kenya and you never know what will happen.

Sure enough, it begins to rain.

But get this! Just as if to exonerate the pastor, a rainbow appears, crossing over the whole sky, and then to top it off, we see a 2nd rainbow right behind it! A double rainbow hanging over the whole sky! You know what? I think this is going to work!

Not to be denied by the rain, we have plugged all the equipment in under a shelter and keep going on with the service. A lady pastor from somewhere in Nairobi wants to be part of this with us, so we give her the microphone to lead the song service. Once we are cranked up and the music is flowing, it lights up the whole area. People are coming from everywhere, dancing in the streets, in the hallways, and out in the open field. Even down the street, a couple of hundred yards away you can see people up in the 3rd and 4th-floor balconies dancing and singing. The kids are all running around having a blast. You should see some of these kids boogie!

All around us is discarded garbage and filth, mud and dirt, but here in the midst of all of it is this spot of truth and light. I have to wonder if these depressing conditions are what makes their rejoicing so intense, or is it just in their nature to embrace life. Whichever it is, they sure know how to praise God.

When it is time for the message, they introduce me as the bishop of this church. (Sigh) I give up. This is a very different culture than ours, and they have different ways of looking at things and different needs, and somehow they need to have someone to look up to.

But although my message is heartfelt and poignant, there is no response from anyone to come to the altar. Now, you have to understand that the loudspeakers have carried this message throughout the whole neighborhood for several blocks, so it's not like they didn't hear it. It just didn't reel any of them in.

I hand the mike to the pastor to close services, and he turns it on! (The preaching, not the microphone). He starts pulling everybody in to come closer and compels them to come to the altar. Over and over, his forcible preaching reaches out and drives them in. Once there, he then brings them into a Sinner's Prayer.

You may feel a bit apprehensive about tactics like this, but it is a measure of how much he believes the Bible and understands the reality of Hell. He is desperate to show them the Truth and bring these people to Salvation and he is not worried about how he does it. This is tricky stuff, but he pulls it off perfectly. As a result, four new souls give their hearts to Jesus.

So much for the bishop! Say what you will, but it's the pastor who got the results, not me.

It takes a long time for us to close down services. Even after the mikes are packed up, souls are still coming up -- some to get saved, some for counseling, some to join this new church, and some for Bibles.

You have to be there to see their faces light up when someone receives their very own Bible. It doesn't seem like that big of a deal to us because we are used to having several Bibles in our homes, and if we want another one, we just go buy it. But for these people, the price of a cheap Bible is the equivalent of a week's wages and there is not a dime to spare – not even for something as precious as a Bible. They either share with others or do without. If they do have a Bible, it is treated with the utmost care because they can't afford another one, and this is the Bread of Life to them.

Their inability to afford a Bible is sharply contrasted with their intense desire for God's Word. They want it desperately, but they just can't reach far enough to get it – and then we come and hand them their very own, personal Bible! You just have to see for yourself what it does to them. I guarantee you, you will never look at a Bible in the same way again. I've spent almost $1,000.00 on Bibles so far, and we are almost out – that's how fast they go, and that's how great the need is – but that doesn't matter because I have already seen how God restores that money to those who have donated to help buy these Bibles. You spend the money, God gives it back to you, and you spend it again. It's a pretty cool system that God has designed.

There are not a lot of extraordinarily great things that I can point to in my life, but this is certainly one of them. I look out over the faces of the souls that we have ministered to and realize that many of these people will now spend eternity in Heaven. The idea that we have been allowed to be a part of that is a very heavy thought indeed.

All this has made us late for the next service somewhere in Nairobi. I have no idea where I am anymore, but it sure isn't someplace that I'd like to take my kids. We worm in and out of broken roads and dimly lit slums with dark alleys and bombed-out dirt roads. People hang out until all hours of the night in these spooky neighborhoods, and it gives it the appearance of some movie set for the Pirates of the Caribbean. In the middle of all this, we arrive at a tiny church lit only by candles. There is no electricity or lights here, so I preach by candlelight.

What really impresses me is that they have sat here for hours on cobbled wooden benches waiting for me, and they don't even know who I am! That's how hungry they are for the Word of God. Granted, they have heard that God has sent a great prophet to preach to them, so there is some real incentive to waiting until I come, but that just serves to make the service all that much better when I finally arrive.

I have given up trying to resist this celebrity status. The more I tell them that I am just a regular guy, the more it becomes proof to them of how humble the Man of God is, which, of course, makes him even greater in their eyes. There is no winning this argument.

Let's face it, you and I both know it's just me, but that's not the point. It's not me that they see – they see Hope. Their situation is so desperate that all they know is that God Almighty has taken notice of their plight and has sent someone special to them. They hang onto every word because God has brought His servant through much trouble from a far distant land to bring His message to them. I suppose that is true. All I know is that the Spirit of God always falls on these services, and everybody is energized and edified – every time, and in every service. That's good enough for me, and I dare not take that hope away from them.

I am convinced that Africa is ripe for revival

because it is like this wherever I go. If there was ever a people whose hearts were open, humble, and hungry, it is these people of Africa. While praying last year, I saw Africa like a savanna of dry grass stretching across the continent. It was so dry that it was yellow and brittle and would crumble at your touch.

All that has to happen is for someone to light a match...

I believe that one of these services in one of these churches a match will be struck that will light a blaze that, once lit, cannot be extinguished, and it will burn across Kenya and then Africa itself.

When the fire falls, I just hope I am there to be part of it.

Thursday, Day 6 – The Orphanage

The Mathare Slum has got to be the darkest pit in Africa. All the slums in Nairobi (and there are several) are bad, but there are elements about Mathare that make it one of the worst hellholes you can imagine.

Mathare is a fairly large area that straddles a small valley in the middle of the city of Nairobi into which are crammed several hundred thousand destitute people. There are no sanitary facilities, no garbage pickup, and no semblance of decency – just mud, trash, and sheets of rusty corrugated tin lashed together to make a mass village of destitution.

The garbage is what you notice first. It is everywhere, even in huge piles where kids play and animals rummage for a meal. You can hardly go through here without seeing someone urinating on the side of a dirt pathway, which makes you wonder what you are stepping through as you negotiate your way through the muck.

10'x10' homes are staked out with sheets of corrugated metal, cardboard, and sticks, crammed against one another like a patchwork of rusty boxes. The corroded tin roofs flow down the hillside to the creek and up the other side. This is like a valley of corrosion and despair.

There is no work or visible means of support to be had other than brewing an illegal, dangerously toxic alcohol down in the polluted creek that runs through the slum. (If the booze doesn't kill you, the water will.) Prostitution, drugs, and crime rule their lives. Although that kind of corruption can be found in any poverty-stricken area, Mathare has the distinction of being controlled by gang-related thugs from some weird cult. (If the thugs don't get you, the hoodoo will.)

Pretty much, you're damned no matter which way you turn. And you're trapped there because there is nowhere else to go, and no way to get there. You are in a whirlpool of despair.

You can just imagine how much sickness and

disease grips this place with AIDS and malnutrition topping the list. The slum is filled with orphans roaming the alleys, digging through the trash, sleeping in the mud, fighting for survival. Almost all of them are HIV positive. That's why they're orphans – their parents died from AIDS and passed it on to them, and nobody – I mean NOBODY—wants to touch them.

Standing in the midst of this are two born-again Christians, Simon and Margaret Mwangi, whom God called to drop their successful careers and start an orphanage in the midst of this hopelessness. This man would comb the alleyways for these HIV-positive orphans and bring them home with him, and God would heal these tiny children of AIDS, rickets, severe malnutrition, and a host of other devastating diseases.

Starting with nothing and without any support from any organization, they created an orphanage based on faith. Today, they have grown to several tiny, dimly lit schoolrooms, teaching, feeding, and caring for not only the orphans that they pick up but also many of the children around them.

I have devoted the entire day to visit their orphanage. This pastor had attended a service I held in Nairobi two years ago, and told me that that service affected him dramatically and galvanized him to the purpose that God had called him to. Apparently, he answered the call because what he and his wife have accomplished is nothing short of miraculous, and I feel humbled just to visit them here.

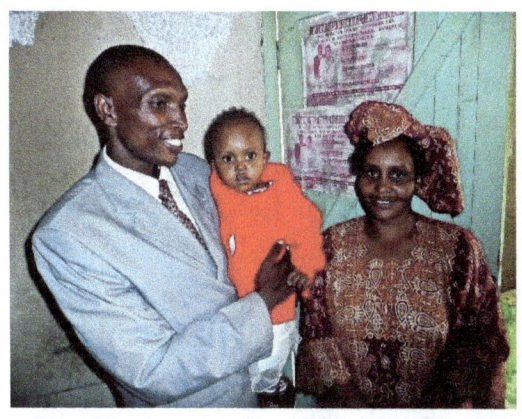

I could write for pages, describing what they have built, the look on the faces of these children, and the strong vision that you can feel just being in the midst of them, but if you haven't walked through the pits of Mathare, you would never really grasp the enormity of this work of God.

I spent the morning visiting all the children in their classrooms. They are so happy to have visitors and have put on a presentation for me. When I look into their faces, I see lives that have been reclaimed from death.

What would their lives have been like right now if these people had not rescued them? That is, if they would have been alive at all. It is an emotional moment for me.

Simon is the driving force that started this work, but as I sit in a tiny room that serves as their kitchen/dining room/ living room, I can look into his wife Margaret's face and see a depth there and the pain of quiet sacrifice that no one knows about, not even her husband. There is something large about her, large and soft. She may have the strength of an iron will to break through the challenges that she has faced, but behind it is a soft heart, big enough to absorb and encompass all these precious little souls that God has sent to her.

I am choked up as I look deep into her eyes and give her a message from the Lord that, although no one else knows, He knows. He has not forgotten, and He will requite her. Man, I feel like I am in the presence of royalty.

Their church has gathered together and is patiently waiting for me to come to the services that have been set up for my arrival. This is a very special time for them, and they have come expecting something special from God. It is in times like these that I wonder what I am doing here because I sure don't feel like I have anything special to offer them. But then, we've already been through that, haven't we?

The service takes on the same pattern and direction that I always go in – worship, preaching out of a passage of Scripture, and prayer. I don't know how long I was preaching because time seemed suspended, but the praying part went on for a long time.

Even if I do not feel anything extraordinary, the people in the congregation do. They are touched by the hand of God. Since I came to minister to them and not to be ministered to, I guess it makes sense that I don't always get to feel all the stuff that they are feeling. At least I think that makes sense.

I don't know if it is their faith, my faith, or just the fever of the moment that has elevated us to another level, but we are floating through time. I have no idea how many people I prayed over, but when we were finally done, the service had lasted 5½ hours, and even then, no one wanted to leave.

Late at night, I work my way back home wondering what will happen next to all these people that I have preached to during the last few days. Will these services change things for them and their churches, or will it just be another bump in the road? Perhaps another revivalist will come along and nudge them again, but it is not likely. I am the first evangelist of any nationality to come and preach in some of these places, and there might not be any after me.

The bishop at the "Lunchtime Service" church told me that although it was admirable that I spent time preaching in these little churches, I really should be spending time in the big churches and national organizations because my message was so important. Yeah, and ignore all the little people, right?. That tells you something about the Kenyan church leadership, doesn't it? While big-time preachers like this bishop are over at the Temple during the Feast days, look for me over at the Pool of Bethesda where the sick, maimed, and poor are lying there hoping for a troubling of the water.

The word "slums" has an ugly connotation, even to those who live in them, but I look at it differently. I would rather be there where the intense need can be felt and where you can hear the sound of hearts desperately crying out for God, than to walk in the clean and polished halls of ivory where the only sound you can hear are empty echoes off of bare marble walls. Jesus seemed to have a similar propensity to hang out in places such as these, while the Pharisees were afraid to touch anything that would make them unclean. Things haven't changed much in 2,000 years.

As usual, I get back to the hotel close to midnight and I am too tired to do anything: read, pray, or write down what happened. Somebody please remind me to slow down the next time I come here.

… Then again, you only live once, right?

Friday, Day 7

I should have known. I should have recognized the signs and realized what was coming. This is old stuff for me, but I just wasn't thinking along those lines of experience – I just thought I was having a bad day.

The day started okay. I met with an apostle from Nigeria in the hotel lobby and I shared what the Lord had shown me for his country. This is the 4th or 5th pastor who has contacted me and offered to help take me throughout Nigeria to share my message with them. Nigeria is next on the list.

The Lord showed me a cloud of thick darkness over Nigeria, especially northern Nigeria. As I looked, I could see little pinpricks of light shining out of the midst of that darkness, and could hear these faint cries for help coming from them. I have to go. I don't know what awaits me there, but I have to go. Nigeria is next. I have no idea where the money will come from, but I have to go.

I told this pastor what the Lord had shown me and it must have struck a chord with him because he offered to host me there while in the capital. This is the 4th pastor, one from each section of Nigeria, who has shown up out of nowhere to help host me in Nigeria. Do you think maybe it's a sign?

As soon as I left him and headed into town, however, I almost got arrested and sent to jail. I was on my way to the Bible Book Store to get some more Bibles, and a cop saw me talking on the cell phone while driving. I could see him running through traffic and I just knew that somehow he was running after me. Oh, great. If this guy resents white people, my goose is cooked.

Sure enough, I'm in trouble. Apparently, not only is talking on a cell phone while driving against the law, it is a serious offense. He gets in and tells me to drive to the Police Station where I will be booked. It's almost like asking you to load the gun that is going to shoot you.

I figure that I had better tell everyone that I will be, uh, a bit delayed, so I begin to reach for the cell phone to call them. Yeah, that's all I need to do, right? Pick up the phone again, this time while driving the cop who is still yelling at me. Thank God, I caught myself before I picked it up. Hey, I never said I was the smartest guy in the class.

I'm not sure, but for some reason, the cop let me go. But now I have to fight for a parking spot in the midday traffic somewhere close enough to the store so I can carry 3 large boxes of Bibles to the car. Going to jail might have been easier. Getting the parking spot in front of the Bible store ranks right up there with parting the Red Sea, but – and I can hardly believe it –a simple prayer of quiet desperation is answered when someone backs out of a parking spot right in front of the store as I pull up. I can't believe it.

Yeah, I know. You're thinking, "So what? What's the big deal?" The big deal is that in the whirlwind of stress and anxiety, God gave me a sign that He is still on my side and listens to my prayers. And right about then, I really needed to know that.

A faithful brother back in the U.S. has told Cindy that he will pay for 500 Bibles. It still chokes me up to think about it. The value in human souls is inestimable and can't be measured in money. You have to see the faces of these people to really understand how huge this is in the eternal scope of things. Somehow, he must know. If he doesn't, he will when he meets these souls face to face in Eternity.

It's time to head back for another Bible reading group and services, but I'm so tired that I am barely able to stay awake. I have to slow down this pace. The level of intensity has been slowly draining me – both the preaching and the driving through traffic – and I have not realized the toll it has been taking. I know I've lost weight because my pants are so loose, I can pull them off me. I feel light and weak like I could float away, but there are only a few more days to go. But everybody wants me to come to their church also and minister, and it is hard to refuse because I will only be here for a limited time. But pretty soon, if I don't get a break, I am not going to be good to anyone. I guess this is what happens when you get old.

Tonight is our last open-air crusade. We have won souls at every open-air meeting and at every place we have preached, the only exception being the "lunch hour services". I haven't counted how many have gotten saved, but it's not the number that is important to me – it's the presence of the Lord to draw them to the altar. I take it as a seal of approval that His Spirit is working in the midst of us.

After ministering to all the new souls, it's off to some tiny shack down on a dark and muddy road in the middle of one of the slums. There are 16 people here, a dirt floor, and a tin roof, but this is where the Holy Ghost takes charge tonight.

Cinch up your pants, take a deep breath, and stand up ready to give it whatever you've got (if I've got anything left). Out of somewhere comes a brand-new message, and I am preaching up a storm. Gone is the fatigue and weakness. The moment I stood up, the Spirit of God took over, and I left my flesh somewhere far behind in the excitement of the Holy Ghost.

I come to the end of an intense message like pulling in the reins on galloping horses and jumping off the saddle. I stood there and all I said was, "Let's pray".

That's all I said, and the Spirit came pouring down in buckets.

We started praying and couldn't stop. We were overwhelmed by the outpouring, swimming in it, lost in its power, drenched in the glory of God. Whenever I thought it would finally slow down and come to an end, it would pour down all over again and knock you back, rolling over you with Holy Laughter.

After a while, I figured that since I was the preacher, I should lay hands on each one and pray over them. Sounds funny, I know, but I wasn't sure what I was supposed to do, and I figured that laying hands on everybody sounded like a pretty good thing to do.

That started things up all over again. People rose up; people fell down; some went down to crumble in prayer, crushed on the floor by the power of the Holy Spirit of God; others fell backward, slain in the Spirit. I didn't know what would happen next, so I went back to the front of the church and sat down and just watched.

A Match in Dry Grass

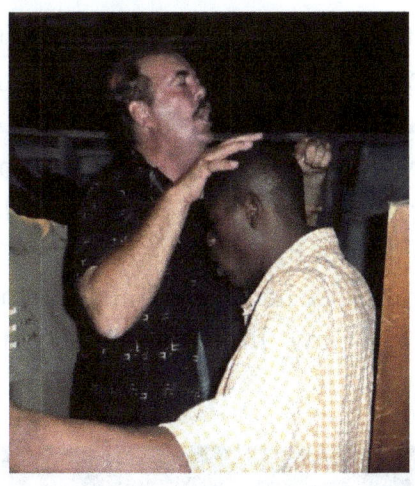

I felt like I was standing on the outside looking in. The presence of God was so thick that it almost looked like a fog had filled the room ... and I'm not so sure that it didn't. As I sat there watching the Spirit of God envelop this church, I had the distinct thought that this might be the match that would light the dry grass of Africa.

I've been waiting all week for this. I knew that this week was going to bring forth something very special, not the ordinary revival services, but something much bigger. At first, I was afraid because you always want to believe that this is the time when the supernatural will happen, but I don't want to be proclaiming the same old nonsense and be another "wannabe". If it is going to happen, it is going to happen, and if not, then it won't. But this time it did happen.

Dalen Garris

I can't tell you what will come of this meeting. Maybe it is just the first of many to follow. Maybe it will start a fire that will catch, and maybe it will go out before it spreads to other churches. I don't know what will happen, but I know that God has a plan, and this meeting was part of that plan.

If nothing else happens while I am in Nairobi, this evening in this tiny little rundown church will be enough.

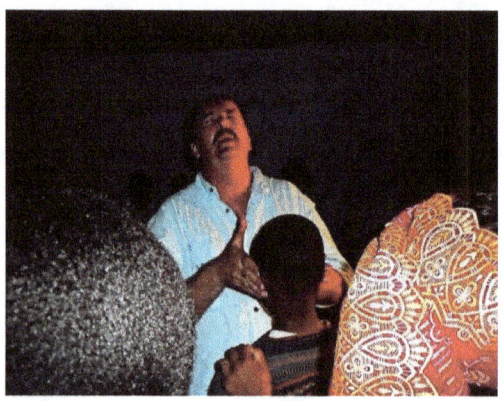

Saturday, Day 8

The other day, I was looking at the flip-flops someone was wearing and noticed how worn-out they were. It's the preferred mode of footwear here – cheap, worn-out flip-flops. Maybe it's because they are so cheap, or maybe it's because they are so easy to wear, but on this side of town, you see them everywhere.

You'd think that these shoes are so cheap that folks would just buy a new pair when they get worn out and throw the old ones away, but they don't. They keep on wearing them. In some ways, these flip-flops are just like the people who wear them. Simple and easy, nothing fancy, and often worn-out.

Perhaps this is why humility comes so easy to them. I was listening to someone preach about Psalm 100, and it struck me that these people are able to grasp what the Psalmist meant when he wrote, "It is He that has made us, and not we ourselves." It takes an abject humility that most people do not possess to understand the fullness of that scripture. In the sophisticated West, we understand it with our heads, but here in Africa, they understand it with their hearts.

Maybe my perspective would change dramatically if I were able to see the other side of town where the standard of living is higher. I hear that there are sections of Nairobi that are very high class with nice stores and great restaurants. That's where all the whites are.

Now that I stop and think about it, I realize that I am the only white guy anywhere around on this side of town. No wonder they think I'm special. I probably glow in the dark!

Today is not a day for preaching and ministering. I have promised to visit both of the people who have hosted me during my past two visits to Kenya. One lives on one side of Nairobi and the other lives miles out of town in the other direction. This will be a day for driving and little else, and I welcome the break.

Of course, driving on the wrong side of the street in a vehicle that is mirror image of what you are used to is not a stress-free break. I'm not sure how I have been able to manage, but it is somehow a testament to the adaptability of human beings. There have been a few close calls, especially when I turn a corner and naturally swing into the side with the oncoming traffic. The Swahili I hear them yell at me has a funny resemblance to the Italian you hear in the traffic in New York.

I've told you about the kamikaze Matatu drivers zooming around, but there is an added road hazard that you will never see anywhere else in the world – the Mokokoteni.

The Mokokoteni are the workhorse turtles of the streets. These are human-drawn carts as wide as a car, mounted on axles with automobile wheels. Two long poles serve as the handles that are used to pull these things through traffic like a coolie with a massive rickshaw.

Out here, if you want anything hauled somewhere, you don't load it up in your pickup truck – there are no pickup trucks here – you get a mokokoteni driver to come by and deliver it for you. It might be dirt or merchandise, bamboo poles, empty barrels, or a pile of rocks – if it needs to be hauled, these guys haul it.

Unfortunately, they haul it right through the middle of traffic. As you're avoiding the matatus dive-bombing you as you rush through traffic, you also have to be careful that you don't run right into one of these mokokoteni, lumbering up the middle of the road right in your lane.

This is a wonderful day for me. I don't have to be anything or anybody today, and that takes a real weight off me. There is much I don't understand about this culture and their spiritual and emotional needs, and some of it has to do with their "tribal chieftain" mentality, the need to look up to someone in charge. At least it seems that way.

And there are always those who are ready to fill the position. It seems everyone around here has to have a title: Pastor, Bishop, Apostle; Butcher, Baker, Candlestick Maker. Funny, there aren't many prophets around, if any at all. At least, I haven't heard of any. Maybe because that's the one office that actually has to do something to prove his position and God-given authority.

There are some stiff warnings in Matthew 23 concerning titles and their abuse. If you have real power and authority in God – the kind that can be felt – then you don't need a title to advertise it. Little letters in front of your name and little letters after it, do not give you authority in God, neither do impressive sounding titles. Jesus' admonition, "…and all ye are brethren", is good enough for me.

Just call me Brother Dale.

Sunday, Day 9

I am sitting here in the hotel late at night reviewing the day's pictures. It's the faces that stare back at me that tug at my heart and say, "I am a real person. Do not forget me." It's not just the kids, who love to ham it up for the camera; it's the adults that reach out a finger to touch my heart. They are the ones who struggle through what life has dealt them and who shoulder the burdens placed upon them with the grim resolution to keep trudging through to the end.

Maybe I'm just melodramatic, or perhaps I feel the contrast between the extreme conditions they live in and what we have in America. It may be that since they have never experienced the difference, it does not affect them that much. They understand the poverty; they just don't understand the contrast.

But there are those who do. They are the ones who have picked up the burden to minister to the others – some to their congregations, others to orphans and the destitute. But although you can see a trace of stooped shoulders from the burdens they carry, you cannot see it in their countenance. It's as if they have the touch of an extra shine given to them from God.

You cannot know the desperate conditions that wrap around their lives, even if you see it for yourself. It is more than the poverty or the unsanitary conditions – it's the dim ray of hope that hangs over them more like a shadow than a light. If they could only reach it, they could pull themselves out, but it is too far for most of them to reach and so they fall back in resignation to the life they have been born into.

Those few who, instead of looking up to lift their own conditions in life, have stooped down to help the others in their destitution are the ones in which you can see an ethereal shine in their eyes. It's hard to describe, and it's not something I have noticed before, but it is most definitely there.

This morning I visited a church in the bowels of the Industrial Area slums. It is like walking into the city dump to find a church made of corrugated tin and wooden poles in the midst of the piles of garbage. As a matter of fact, there is a whole community that has been built here, complete with stores, kiosks selling phone cards, kids playing in the heaps of trash, chickens, a wandering pig, and a set of railroad tracks running down the middle.

I have been communicating with this pastor for the last few months and have been waiting for this opportunity to meet him. He is young but strong. His vision for God is set in stone, and his resolute determination to break through obstacles can be felt when you shake his hand. He is a winner.

Since I am early, I am able to talk to many of the people and ministers who have come to church, and I am impressed with their understanding of the difference between the modern Gospel that is broadcast over TV and the bedrock realities of the old-fashioned Gospel that they know is true. Not only do I not have to tell them anything, but they are also listening to every word to see which Gospel I subscribe to.

Well, you know me, I'm hellfire on wheels, which doesn't work so well in the States, but they love it here. I guess I passed the test because they are genuinely happy to see me. The services are loaded with pastors, bishops, and other ministers that have come all over Nairobi to hear me. Some have been at churches that I have preached at, but many of the others have only heard of me from others. All of them are here for the same thing: they want to be energized, driven, and goaded on to see a real move of God, even if it means being reproved. They have not come to be flattered; they have come to hear the Truth.

My message is always the same: the price of revival, turning the focus from themselves to others, repentance and determination, and what it takes to walk in the Spirit of God – all basic stuff. Someone has called me a "Revivalist", and I guess that sums it up, but it is not the message, but it is the Spirit of God that falls on every one of these services that makes the difference between church and revival. That is what they are here for.

This service is no different. I challenge them with a strong altar call for repentance before they can ever have the revival they so desperately want, and then I turn it over to the pastor. Slowly, but steadily, they start coming until the whole church, bishops and all, are at the altar, hands raised, faces bowed low, crying out to God. You can hear them pray from a half-mile away. This is serious stuff.

Twenty minutes later they are still praying, and you can feel a cleansing in the air like something has washed through this church and released some heavy burdens. It's hard to describe on paper what the supernatural presence of God is like and to compress the intensity of that experience into a short paragraph to be casually read by someone passing by. All I know is that something happened here that was a pretty big deal, and I thank God that I got to be a part of this.

My biggest regret is that Cindy and the girls aren't here to experience this with me. The rest of you guys can go get your own plane tickets here, but somehow I want my family to see this instead of just hearing the tales second-hand. The thing that cannot be relayed in print or pictures is the presence of the Holy Spirit. How do you tell someone what it feels like to be lifted up and enveloped in it?

(Sigh) I guess you just have to come to see for yourselves.

I have been here for 7 hours (Yeah. Try that back home sometime.), and they are coming back for another service in a couple of hours, but I am off to preach at my farewell service in the church we just planted in Kariobungi. That is if I can drag myself out of here.

There are several folks waiting to have a word of prayer with me before I leave. Each one has a poignant tale to tell. These people inspire me with their selfless vision for others. A couple have orphanages, others have churches, and sometimes several churches, but all of them have taken on challenges that are much bigger than themselves. These are burdens that only God can place upon you because you could never handle them on your own. They want the man of God to pray over them so that God will help them shoulder those burdens and bring them to a place of victory.

When I look into some of their eyes, the Lord shows me depths of soul that are beyond the natural. These are heroes in God, invested with uncommon courage and strength, separated by God to take on the impossible with nothing but their faith to drive them on. They look at me as someone special sent from God, but as I lay hands on them I feel I am in the presence of royalty, that in the not too distant future, when I am walking by their mansions with some of my friends, I will be proud to point out that I knew them here.

I leave deeply affected. I pray that they have also been affected and will take what has happened to them during this service and spread a fire in their own ministries. This is how it works – someone strikes a match, and others carry the torch.

Back in Kariobungi, I am thrilled to see that the

original 4 or 5 members in our little church have multiplied in one week to over 25. The three friends who have started this church are the pillars upon which this church will stand, and I have no doubts that they will do what it takes to make this not only work but prosper.

I feel like Paul saying goodbye to the Ephesians, and they feel the same way. The members here don't know me, but it feels like I am saying goodbye to close friends that I have known for years. It kinda gets me that even though I barely know them, they are going to miss me. I'm not sure how to handle that because I am normally a cranky old man with a bad attitude and am not affected by all this warm, fuzzy stuff. But this is really getting to me. Maybe I'm just getting soft in my old age.

This was my last service in Kenya. I am completely drained: physically and spiritually. I have preached somewhere between 20 to 30 messages in these 10 days, and I have that "finished" feeling that tells me that I have accomplished what God has sent me here to do. I don't know how many lives have been touched, and how many have been transformed. I can only give them to God to hold them in His hands of mercy and let Him bring them to that place that He intended for them all along. I was just a nudge in that direction.

In the beginning, I honestly feared that this trip might be a vain waste of money to minister to a small handful of people, that nothing significant would really come out of it, and that I would end up being not much more than a fraud. I guess that was the devil. (You think?) I may never know what was accomplished here, but I have this sense that it was far greater than my expectations. Years from now, strong oak trees will be towering over the landscape whose seeds were planted during these 10 days. Fruit will grow and create more fruit which will, in turn, spread across Nairobi and Kenya, and who knows, maybe even the world.

Something happened here that I can feel but not describe in words. What does this all mean for the rest of us? Should everyone jump on a plane and run to some

3rd world country? Of course not, but maybe we need to see a reflection of our hearts in all this.

Life is good in America, but we lack something in our souls that these people are rich in. Their existence may be threadbare, but their hearts are open to God in a way that is not possible when your life is satiated. They have the true riches that cannot be measured in new cars, beautiful homes, and all the conveniences of life. You can see it in their eyes, feel it in their hearts, and hear it in their crying out to God.

Theirs will last when ours are long gone.

Monday, Day 10

Today is the day that I'm going home! I've purposely left this day free because I know that somehow it won't stay free; somebody or something will show up. Still, I am going to sneak out of the hotel and scurry away before anyone calls me or shows up. I'm tired and I'm drained. I don't' think I have anything left in me to give out, so I'm not going to be good to anyone right now anyway.

Before I can make a clean breakaway, however, the day's schedule begins to fill up. (I told you.) I have to stop back at the Mathare orphanage to pick up a DVD of our visit there.

But there is another visit I must make before leaving. A pastor has been calling me for days, begging me to please not leave until I visit his church, or at least meet with him at his office. I have no idea who he is or how he knows me, but I get this feeling that I need to do this one last thing before the Lord will release me to go home.

This pastor attended a service/seminar that I had two years ago, and it inspired him to start his own church. Like I have done with so many other pastors, I promise him that I will come and minister to his congregation when I return. It's going to have to be a month-long trip the next time just to visit all the churches that are anticipating my return. I guess that means I am coming back.

But for now, I am on my way home. I can't tell

you how much I am ready to go home. The whole trip will take well over 30 hours, and I just want to hurry up and get started.

At the airport, I run into a group from Dallas, Texas. And not just from Dallas, but they are with some people from the Ferris Ave Baptist Church in Waxahachie. Small world indeed. They are all excited to be in an exotic foreign land, but I am so weary that I feel like an old road warrior on the long road home. It has been a long 10 days.

Conclusion

I'm not sure why the Lord put Kenya in my life, but each trip here has been more powerful than the one before. I started with nothing – no money, no church behind me, and no idea of what I was doing or what the message was – and it has grown into a major ministry. While I am an unknown in the States, I seem to have become a small celebrity in Kenya. You just never know what the Lord will do in your life if you let Him.

I believe that this trip was more than just another exercise in Christian ministry. If that was the case, we could just send another youth group from our churches and they would do a fine job. There is something more than that going on here. I believe that Kenya is on the verge of a great move of God, but there are a few obstacles in the way.

They are starving for God, and they are willing to do whatever it takes, but I get this feeling that while they are bending as far as they can, they are not breaking yet. They need that extra snap to bring them into that brokenness down deep in their souls that always precedes any great revival from God. But they are almost there.

There are two other obstacles that must be overcome: that "welfare mentality" idea of a Gospel of Entitlement, and their Tribal Chieftain mentality.

My message has repeatedly been that the Gospel is not about us; it's about others. They, have gotten this idea of a Gospel of Entitlement from the American prosperity preachers on TV, i.e., "What's in it for me?", "Bless me, bless me, bless me, God." Their focus has to change. If they do not, it will be impossible for revival to break out because revival is all about sacrifice so that others can be saved. The good news is, however, that more and more of them are becoming disillusioned with what they see on Christian broadcasting and are coming back to that old-fashioned Gospel and the path that leads to the Cross.

The other obstacle, the Tribal Chieftain mentality, is a mindset that swings both ways. For one, they have to get rid of the idea that the church pastors and leaders are royalty and that laymen cannot attain to that level. That idea has hampered the Body of Christ by setting up false echelons and maintaining a class structure in the Church that does not exist in the Spirit of God.

But that mentality also swings the other way. The members of the congregation must also get rid of the idea that the pastors are supposed to do all the work. Fire burns up, not down. If revival does not burn in the pews, it won't burn in the streets. If we wait for the pastors to do all the work while we sit and wait for God to drop a revival in our laps, we will wait forever.

When I bring these messages forth, it is as if they received an epiphany. They don't mind working; they just don't know what to do. Once they realize that not only does God not place limitations on them, but also holds them responsible, it sets them free.

All the elements are here for revival to break out. In one of these churches during one of their services, a match will be struck, and once it is lit, the fire will start.

I believe that. Any obstacles in the way will come down quickly.

I think back to that panic attack that I had when I first arrived 10 days ago and laugh. It has not only been worth the effort and expense, but we have won victories that will last for a long time. There is no telling what has been accomplished here. I am leaving feeling victorious, full, and accomplished. I have done what I was sent to do.

Now it is their turn to grab the opportunity given them and finish the job.

About the Author

Dalen Garris has been in ministry since 1970 during the Jesus Movement in California. In 1997, he began a radio broadcast that spread to dozens of countries, from Israel and Saudi Arabia to Africa and the Philippines. His program, *Fire in the Hole*, was broadcast four times a week for several years across North America on the Sky Angel network as the Voice of Jerusalem.

A newspaper column followed, for which he has written over 700 articles, which have been published in local newspapers and Christian magazines in several countries. He has also written over a dozen books and several booklets.

Since 2004, he has been lighting the fires of revival in churches spread across sub-Saharan Africa. During the course of 17 years, he has preached in over 1,000 churches and has seen hundreds of them set on fire and explode with growth. Hundreds of new ones have been planted across Africa. Hundreds of people have been supernaturally healed during the healing lines, and tens of thousands have been saved.

And the fires are still burning.

Because of his work across Africa, Dalen Garris was awarded an honorary Doctorate in 2017 by the Northwestern Christian University of Florida.

Dalen Garris

Dr. Garris currently lives with Cindy, his wife of 44 years, in Waxahachie and is still heavily involved with churches across Africa. His pressing hope is in seeing this powerful move of God in Africa ignite us here in America. He believes that this upcoming generation will be the Gideon Generation that will usher in this last, great revival that he has preached about for so many years.

If you would like Dalen Garris to speak at your church or organization, please contact us for times and schedules. We do not charge, nor will we ever charge, to preach the Gospel anywhere in the world.

Books by Dalen Garris:

Available at: www.Revivalfre.org/books

Revival Books
- Four Steps to Revival
- Do You Have Eternal Security?
- Standing in the Gap
- Two Covenants
- Fire in the Hole

Revival Campaigns
- The Kenya Diaries
- A Trumpet in Nigeria
- A Scent of Rain
- Into the Heart of Darkness
- Fire and Rain
- Revival Campaigns in Africa – 2019
- The Battle for Nigeria
- A Match in Dry Grass
- A Light in the Bush

A Voice in the Wilderness series:
- vol. 1, the Journey Begins
- vol. 2, the Early Years
- vol. 3, Prophet Rising
- vol. 4, Revival in the Wings
- vol. 5, Sound of an Abundance of Rain
- vol. 6, Watchman, What of the Night?
- vol. 7, Mud and Heroes
- vol. 8, Ashes in the Morning
- vol. 9, Shaking the Olive Tree

www.ingramcontent.com/pod-product-compliance
Lightning Source LLC
Chambersburg PA
CBHW070451050426
42451CB00015B/3432